Love Is a Special Way of Feeling

Silver Anniversary Edition

JOAN WALSH ANGLUND

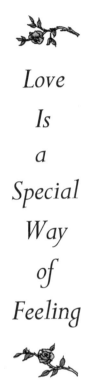

Love

Is

a

Special

Way

of

Feeling

Harcourt Brace Jovanovich, Publishers

San Diego   New York   London

BY JOAN WALSH ANGLUND

Request for permission to make copies
of any part of the work should be mailed to:
Permissions, Harcourt Brace Jovanovich, Publishers,
Orlando, Florida 32887

Printed in the United States of America

Library of Congress Cataloging in Publication Data

Anglund, Joan Walsh.
Love is a special way of feeling.

Reprint. Originally published: New York : Harcourt, Brace, 1960.
Summary: Words and illustrations describe the tender,
happy feeling that is called love.
[1. Love—Fiction] I. Title. PZ7.A586Lq 1985 [Fic] 84-19296
ISBN 0-15-249724-2

Silver Anniversary Edition

A B C D E

HBJ

with love,
for
margaret
julian
helen

Love is a special way of feeling. . . .

It is the safe way we feel
when we sit on our mother's
lap with her arms around us
tight and close.

It is the good way we feel
when we talk to someone
and they want to listen
and don't tell us to go away
and be quiet.

It is the happy way we
feel when we save a
bird that has been hurt . . .

or feed a lost cat . . .

or calm a frightened colt.

Love is found in unexpected places. . . .
It is there in the quiet moment
when we first discover
a beautiful thing . . .
when we watch a bird
soar high against
a pale blue sky . . .

when we see a lovely flower
that no one else has noticed . . .

when we find a place
that shelters us and is
all our very own.

Love starts in little ways. . . .
It may begin the day
we first share our
thoughts with someone else . . .

or help someone who needs us. . . .

Or, sometimes, it begins
because, even without words,
we understand how someone feels.

Love comes quietly . . .
but you know when it is there,
because, suddenly . . .
you are not alone any more . . .
and there is no sadness
inside you.